HUBBLE DEEP FIELD

HOW A PHOTO REVOLUTIONIZED OUR UNDERSTANDING OF THE UNIVERSE

by Don Nardo

Content Adviser: Frank Summers, PhD
Outreach Astrophysicist
Space Telescope Science Institute

COMPASS POINT BOOKS
a capstone imprint

Compass Point Books are published by Capstone,
1710 Roe Crest Drive, North Mankato, Minnesota 56003
www.mycapstone.com

Editor: Catherine Neitge
Designers: Tracy Davies McCabe and Catherine Neitge
Media Researcher: Svetlana Zhurkin
Library Consultant: Kathleen Baxter
Production Specialist: Laura Manthe

Image Credits
Alamy: Pictorial Press Ltd., 17, 56; Courtesy of Dr. Robert Williams, 27, 29; ESA/
NASA/Hubble, 35, 40–41; Getty Images: Corbis/VCG/Roger Ressmeyer, 21, The
LIFE Picture Collection/J.R. Eyerman, 19, 57 (right); iStockphoto: rappensuncle,
22; NASA: 5, 9, 10, 11, 25, 39, 51, 57 (left), R. Williams (STScI) and the Hubble
Deep Field Team, 13, 58 (right), STScI/Hubblesite, 48; NASA/ESA: H. Teplitz and M.
Rafelski (IPAC/Caltech), A. Koekemoer (STScI), R. Windhorst (ASU), Z. Levy (STScI),
50, Holland Ford (JHU), the ACS Science Team, 49, Hubble, 38, J. Lotz (STScI), 55,
59 (right), M. Postman and D. Coe (STScI), and the CLASH Team, 53, M. Robberto
(STScI/ESA) and the Hubble Space Telescope Orion Treasury Project Team, 43, P.
van Dokkum (Yale University), S. Patel (Leiden University), and the 3D-HST Team,
45, Robert Williams and the Hubble Deep Field Team (STScl), cover, 31, S. Beckwith
(STScI) and the HUDF Team, 58 (left), Z. Levay (STScI/AURA), 37, Z. Levay, STScI,
Moon image T. Rector, I. Dell'Antonio/NOAO/AURA/NSF, 47; Shutterstock: AuntSpray,
24, Cezary Stanislawski, 23, 59 (left), Denis Belitsky, 6, isak55, 7, Marcel Clemens,
15, Viktar Malyshchyts, 33

Library of Congress Cataloging-in-Publication Data
Names: Nardo, Don, 1947-
Title: Hubble Deep Field : how a photo revolutionized our understanding of the
universe / by Don Nardo.
Description: North Mankato, Minnesota : Compass Point Books, a Capstone imprint,
[2018] | Series: Captured science history | Audience: Age 10-12. | Audience: Grade 4
to 6. | Includes bibliographical references and index.
Identifiers: LCCN 2017010280| ISBN 9780756556433 (library binding) | ISBN
9780756556471 (paperback) | ISBN 9780756556518 (ebook pdf)
Subjects: LCSH: Hubble Space Telescope (Spacecraft) | Astronomy—Pictorial Works—
Juvenile literature. | Deep space—Pictorial works—Juvenile literature.
Classification: LCC QB500.268 .N37 2018 | DDC 523.1—dc23
LC record available at https://lccn.loc.gov/2017010280

Printed in the United States of America.
010374F17

TABLEOFCONTENTS

ChapterOne
BOLD HUNT FOR DISTANT GALAXIES

Astronomer Bob Williams and his scientific team prepared to take a big risk in December 1995, a risk that could have ended Williams' distinguished career as a scientist. It involved taking a series of photographs. Williams was keenly aware that there was great power in certain photos. Still fresh in his mind was the Blue Marble—a magnificent portrait of Earth taken from high above by U.S. astronauts in 1972. It had caught the attention of people around the globe, showing that they lived on a tiny, fragile sphere floating in the vastness of space.

Williams wanted to capture a very different sort of image—one of an area of space extremely far away from our planet. Two years before, he had become director of the Space Telescope Science Institute (STScI), which ran the National Aeronautics and Space Administration's Hubble Space Telescope. Launched into space in 1990, NASA's Hubble held out the promise of clearly seeing cosmic objects so distant that they appeared dim and blurry from ground-based telescopes.

Williams wanted to point Hubble at a tiny patch of sky near the handle of the Big Dipper, in the constellation Ursa Major, the Great Bear. The patch covers an area as big as a grain of sand held at arm's

Apollo 17 **astronauts snapped a photo of Earth in 1972 that became known as the Blue Marble.**

length. The plan was to take hundreds of pictures of the target area during 10 days. Sophisticated computer software would combine them into a single image.

The goal was almost too ambitious to imagine. Williams and his team wanted to test the outer limits of space and time. We know that the speed of light is 186,000 miles (300,000 kilometers) per second. The light from a very distant galaxy travels at that speed. So if the light has been traveling for millions

The Milky Way galaxy, which contains our solar system, fills the night sky.

of years, glimpsing the object now is in a very real way seeing back in time at what it looked like when the light began its journey. Williams and a small group of colleagues wanted to look for distant galaxies. A galaxy is a gigantic system of millions or billions of stars. Our local galaxy—the one that contains the sun—is the Milky Way. Many other galaxies exist beyond the Milky Way. Hundreds of thousands of these massive systems were detected and photographed in the 20th century.

Hubble's camera pointed near the handle of the Big Dipper, a star pattern in the constellation Ursa Major, the Great Bear.

But astronomers had yet to determine how far into the reaches of deep space galaxies existed. They also wondered when the first galaxies appeared. Have they always looked like they do today, or have their shapes evolved over time? And will they, along with the universe itself, go on expanding forever? Williams and his team hoped that photographing some very distant galaxies might allow them to begin to answer some of these questions.

Using Earth-based telescopes, that little piece of space in Ursa Major appeared to be mostly black and empty of cosmic objects. It contained a few stars known to be in one of the Milky Way's outer arms. Telescopes had also detected a handful of tiny, blurry blobs of light in the target region, which might be galaxies. But if so, there were not many of them. Otherwise, the area Williams had singled out seemed to be composed mostly of empty space.

Considering these facts, several of Williams' fellow astronomers felt that devoting 10 days of Hubble's time to such a venture might be a serious mistake. There was wide agreement that every minute of Hubble's time was scientifically valuable, even precious. What if, after the 10 days, Williams' proposed photo showed mostly empty space?

Further complicating matters was the fact that Hubble already had gained a reputation for not living up to expectations. Not long after the telescope's launch, its first photos had been a disappointment. An unexpected flaw in its mirror had caused the pictures to be blurry.

A group of astronauts from the space shuttle *Endeavour* had saved the day by repairing the space telescope and fixing the problem. But the effort had been costly, and both politicians and the public were now sensitive about projects that might waste Hubble's valuable time. Not surprisingly, some of

Astronauts repaired Hubble's faulty mirror in December 1993.

Williams' colleagues urged him not to move forward with his plan. Some strongly warned him that if his 10-day experiment failed, it might be a public relations nightmare for Hubble and NASA. One of them, Lyman Spitzer Jr., a physicist and astronomer,

PICKING THE PATCH

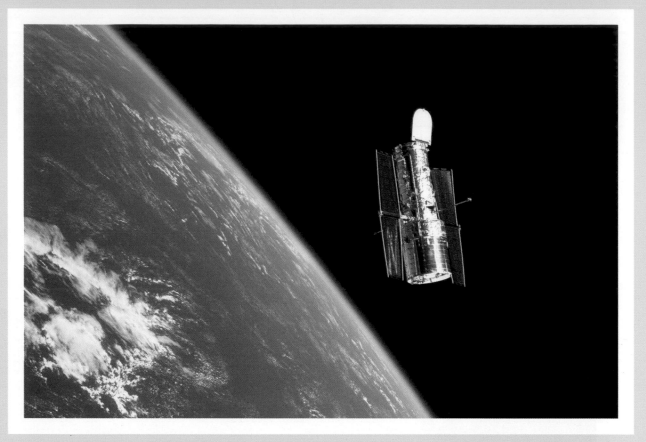

The Hubble Space Telescope floats gracefully above Earth.

Some technical problems had to be overcome in order to take the Hubble Deep Field (HDF) photograph. One was getting around the many stars and other objects in the Milky Way in order to see galaxies lying far outside our local galaxy. Bob Williams and the other scientists who helped him take the HDF solved this problem by choosing a tiny patch of sky in the constellation Ursa Major. Because of the location, only a handful of stars inside the Milky Way would block the view of deep space.

The target patch was also chosen because it is in a continuous viewing zone in relation to the Hubble Space Telescope's orbit. Such a zone is a place in the sky where the space telescope can see and take photographs without Earth's getting in the way. Williams and his colleagues realized that NASA had already eliminated the problem of taking long-exposure photos from a space platform moving at high speeds. As Earth travels around the sun, views from the planet of various objects in space are constantly changing. Because Hubble is in Earth's orbit, whatever spot in the sky it sees also appears to be constantly and quickly changing position.

How, then, could astronomers keep Hubble's onboard camera focused on a spot long enough to take a long-exposure picture? NASA scientists overcame this challenge by developing sophisticated computer software. It compares the position of the target spot in the sky with certain guide stars and calculates tiny course corrections for the camera several times per second. Once the camera is locked on the guide stars, Hubble would barely wobble off its target. According to a NASA book about the space telescope, it is like "holding the beam of a laser pointer all day on the face of a dime located 200 miles away."

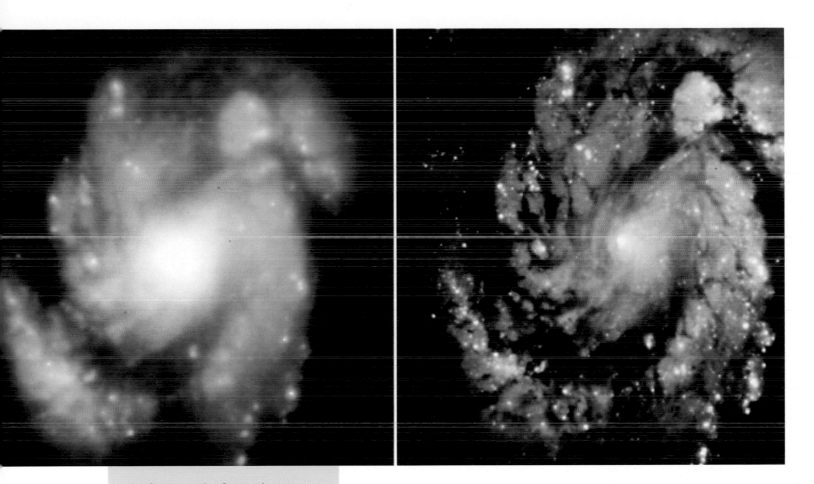

Before and after photos of the galaxy M100 show the dramatic improvement in the Hubble Space Telescope's view of the universe after the 1993 repair mission.

was more diplomatic. "Bob, are you sure you want to do this?" he cordially asked.

But regardless of how many other scientists cautioned Williams, he continued on. He believed that the proposed photo would reveal at least some galaxies. Now that Hubble's optics were as good as new, he reasoned, they might be able to pick up the light of faint galaxies.

In fact, bursting with a spirit of exploratory zeal, Williams was willing to go full speed ahead no matter what the consequences might be. "If you're going to make advances in science," he later said, "you must take risks. I was well aware of the possible consequences if we were to obtain no results. So I was prepared, if necessary, to turn in my resignation."

There was another reason that Williams felt comfortable moving forward with his bold hunt for distant galaxies. As director of the STScI, he was allowed to schedule a certain amount of time to use Hubble for personal projects. "The telescope allocation committee would never have approved such a long, risky project," he said later. "But as director, I had 10 percent of the telescope time, and I could do what I wanted."

So Williams and his team began preparing in earnest to aim Hubble's great orbiting eye at a tiny piece of dark sky in the Great Bear. They knew that the galactic snapshot they sought to create would be composed of more than 340 separate images. Each of those would require an exposure time of up to 40 minutes. Simple math revealed that this would tie up Hubble for quite a number of its revolutions around the planet—roughly 150 orbits in all.

When Hubble's onboard camera began taking the photos on December 18, 1995, Williams and his associates wondered whether the images would show anything significant. If they did not, the public would likely never hear about this astronomical experiment. And Bob Williams might thereafter be known among scientists as learned and well-meaning, but largely

The Hubble Deep Field photo revealed galaxies never seen before.

a dreamer. No one involved foresaw the immense significance of what they were creating. One scientist later said that viewing the result of their efforts— the photo known as the Hubble Deep Field—was "profound." It was, he added, "the most important image humanity had ever taken."

Chapter Two

TO THE EDGE OF THE UNIVERSE

The taking of the now famous Hubble Deep Field photo in 1995 seemed to crown a century already crowded with momentous scientific achievements. Several astronomical developments were related to the questions astronomer Bob Williams sought to answer in creating that now-famous image of distant galaxies.

Many giants of modern astronomy worked in the 20th century. Prominent among them was the brilliant Edwin Hubble, for whom the Hubble Space Telescope was named. He and other gifted researchers explained what galaxies are and revealed a vast universe filled with them. By studying how galaxies moved, astronomers were able to figure out how and about when the universe was born. They also learned about the cosmic time machine. When people see very distant galaxies, they are looking far back into the past, well before our star—the sun—came into being. These and other related facts blazed a trail that later led to the creation of the Hubble Deep Field.

At the same time, a separate trail was being created by using increasingly powerful telescopes. They made it possible for Edwin Hubble and other pioneers of astronomy to accomplish what they did.

Radio telescopes observe the Milky Way. Radio waves from space were first detected in the 1930s.

Production of the increasingly effective telescopes reached a peak in 1990 with the launch of the Hubble Space Telescope.

Meanwhile, the man who would create the Hubble Deep Field was carving out his own path. Born in 1940, when scientists like Edwin Hubble were rocking the scientific world, Bob Williams steadily headed toward the field of astronomy. The Hubble Deep Field became a reality, therefore, thanks to the convergence of three separate paths—one taken by the science of astronomy, the second by rapid telescope advances, and the third by Williams himself.

The path taken by astronomy during the 20th century featured exciting discoveries, including many relating to galaxies and the age and expansion of the universe. In the early 1900s, astronomers still labored in what today seems like a dark age regarding the universe's age and structure. In those days, the term "galaxy" referred strictly to the Milky Way. Many astronomers thought other galaxies might exist, but they had no observable evidence to prove it.

Making this situation even odder, from a modern viewpoint, was the fact that the early cosmic investigators actually could see other galaxies. They simply did not realize what they were seeing. Since the 1700s, astronomers had noticed several faint, foglike patches of light in the night sky. Clearly they were not stars, which look like sharp points of light. For want of a better name, experts named these blurry patches nebulae, from a Latin word meaning "mist" or "cloud."

For a long time, most astronomers thought every nebula was a gaseous cloud floating in space. At least that is what nebulae looked like through the most powerful telescopes that then existed. The main difficulty was that no one could figure out how far away these "clouds" were. Most scientists generally assumed that they were somewhere in the Milky Way. That made sense to them because they thought the Milky Way was the entire universe.

The idea that every nebula was in the Milky Way

received its first major challenge around 1920. The Hooker Telescope—then considerably larger than any before it—began operation atop Mount Wilson in southern California. While studying astronomy at the University of Chicago, Edwin Hubble had done his doctoral dissertation on the nebulae. He used the Hooker Telescope to study the objects. To his surprise, he detected individual stars within several of them.

Studies of these stars permitted Hubble to calculate the distances of the nebulae from Earth. He was stunned to find that they were extremely distant—so far, in fact, that they lay well outside the Milky Way. It was now clear to him and other astronomers that many of the nebulae were not merely nearby floating gas clouds. Instead, they were independent galaxies lying well beyond the Milky Way. The long dark age in the understanding of galaxies and the universe had finally lifted.

Hubble and his colleagues realized that the dramatic revelations about the galaxies could mean only one thing. They meant that the universe was far bigger than previously thought—perhaps 100 or more times larger. (Today it is known to be 250,000 times larger.) Furthermore, the cosmos was not simply sitting still in one spot, as had long been assumed. Instead, studies of the galaxies completed in the 1930s, 1940s, and 1950s by Hubble and others revealed that the galaxies appeared to be moving swiftly through space.

Moreover, all of the galaxies observed seemed to be moving away. From these observations, Hubble and other astronomers concluded that the universe is expanding in all directions. The edges of space seemed to be moving farther and farther outward.

Still another old assumption about galaxies and the cosmos that astronomers overturned was the idea that the Milky Way is at the universe's center.

REVOLUTIONARY EDWIN HUBBLE

One of the 20th century's greatest astronomers, Edwin Hubble, was born November 20, 1889, in Marshfield, Missouri. He studied astronomy at the University of Chicago and while still a student there was invited to help in the final stages of construction of the Hooker Telescope at California's Mount Wilson Observatory. When completed, the telescope was the world's largest. After receiving his doctorate in astronomy, Hubble served briefly as a soldier in World War I. In the early 1920s he started working at Mount Wilson.

One of Hubble's main interests as a young astronomer was studying the Milky Way galaxy, which scientists then thought enclosed the entire universe. Using the mighty Hooker telescope, he detected individual stars in some of the many seemingly gaseous nebulae visible in the night sky. He was able to approximate their distances, which led him to the momentous realization that they were galaxies far outside the Milky Way. He demonstrated that the best-known nebula—in the constellation Andromeda—was a separate galaxy at least 900,000 light-years from the Milky Way. (It was later shown to be almost 2.5 million light-years away.) In 1929 Hubble and astronomer Milton Humason published their research indicating that the other galaxies are moving away from one another. Hubble continued to work at Mount Wilson, as well as at the Mount Palomar Observatory in California, with its 200-inch (5-meter) telescope, until his death at age 63 in September 1953.

His work in astronomy is still hailed as brilliant and revolutionary. Hubble showed that the cosmos is far larger than previously thought, that it is made up of untold numbers of galaxies, and that it is rapidly expanding.

Edwin Hubble posed inside the workings of the huge telescope at Mount Palomar in 1950.

Even after the discovery of galaxies outside the local one, this idea appeared to hold true. After all, it did look to observers on Earth as if the outside galaxies were speeding away in all directions.

Edwin Hubble, however, proposed that this was only an illusion. Whether one lives in the Milky Way or any other galaxy, he explained, one would have the impression that all other galaxies are moving away from that galaxy. Baking a raisin cake became a popular way to illustrate this phenomenon. "Put a raisin cake in the oven, and it's very small," Princeton University astronomer Neta Bahcall wrote. "Then you let it go, and the distance between the raisins is like the distance between the galaxies—it gets larger and larger with time." Furthermore, no matter which raisin one observes from, all other raisins are moving away.

Another theory about the universe developed directly out of the observation of ever-expanding galaxies. Some astronomers theorized that at a point in the dim past, a huge explosion had occurred. The explosion threw outward the material that eventually would become galaxies. In 1949 astronomer Fred Hoyle ridiculed the idea and coined the term "Big Bang" to describe the theory's idea of a cosmic explosion. But in the 1960s significant proof for Big Bang began to accumulate, and even Hoyle came to accept the idea.

A crucial step in the process that led to Hubble's

"Put a raisin cake in the oven, and it's very small. Then you let it go, and the distance between the raisins is like the distance between the galaxies—it gets larger and larger with time."

The Hooker Telescope at Mount Wilson was key to Edwin Hubble's discoveries about the universe.

first observations, which set all the discoveries in motion, was the construction of the Hooker Telescope on Mount Wilson, in California. Its primary mirror, which was 100 inches (2.5 m) wide, gathered far more light than the mirrors and lenses of earlier telescopes. That allowed Hubble and other scientists to see fainter objects and smaller details, including the individual stars in the nebulae.

The powerful Hale Telescope is operated by the California Institute of Technology.

Astronomers, of course, were not satisfied with 100-inch telescopes. Throughout the rest of the century, telescope building rapidly accelerated, creating instruments that let astronomers see farther and farther into space. The Hale Telescope, with a mirror 200 inches (5 m) across, became operational on California's Mount Palomar in 1948. Although

Each of the twin Keck telescopes in Hawaii weighs 300 tons (272 metric tons).

it remained the world's most powerful telescope for years, other huge visual instruments were in the works. The first large multiple-mirror telescope (MMT) appeared at Whipple Observatory in Arizona in 1979. Another MMT duo soon surpassed it. The twin W.M. Keck telescopes sit atop Hawaii's Mount Mauna Kea. Both telescopes have primary reflective surfaces made of 36 mirrors. A computer system coordinates all 36 mirrors, causing them to act like two huge mirrors that are each 33 feet (10 m) across.

But no matter how big ground-based telescopes have become, they all have one drawback. They are on Earth's surface. That means astronomers have to

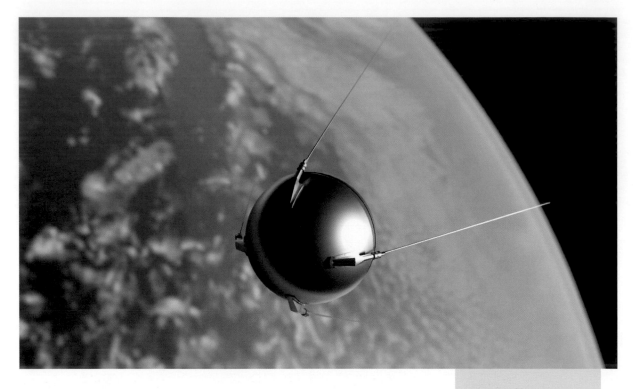

look through miles of atmosphere, which limits how much detail they can see.

That limitation inspired some astronomers to propose building a telescope in space, beyond the distorting atmosphere. A German scientist, Hermann Oberth, suggested in 1923 that such an instrument be created. Lyman Spitzer, an American astrophysicist, discussed the subject in a 1946 article. Yet in those days the idea of building a space telescope seemed like science fiction. Not until the 1960s—several years after the "space age" began with the successful launch of the Russian satellite *Sputnik I*—did NASA officials seriously consider creating an orbiting telescope.

Of course, it was widely recognized that such an

The Hubble Space Telescope was launched in April 1990 on the space shuttle *Discovery.*

instrument would be extremely expensive. For that reason, planning for a space telescope was delayed, and not until 1977 did the U.S. Congress approve the idea. As the project went forward, NASA's leaders decided to name the telescope after Edwin Hubble, to honor his contributions to the knowledge of galaxies and the universe's structure and age.

The Hubble Space Telescope, launched into orbit in 1990, has revolutionized research in astronomy. One of its earliest and most significant results was the Hubble Deep Field photo in 1995. Astronomers were ready to take that step thanks to nearly a century of discoveries about the nature of galaxies, the expanding universe, and the birth of the cosmos. Hubble's distinction as the first major telescope located above Earth's atmosphere made it the only instrument that could do the job.

The third key element in the creation of the Hubble Deep Field—Bob Williams—reached that scientific juncture at the height of a decades-long love affair with astronomy. Born in Dunsmuir, California, in 1940, Williams knew nearly nothing about planets and stars until he was 12. Then he took a science course that included such topics as chemistry, biology, botany, and astronomy.

Williams recalls that the astronomy unit interested him enough to inspire a trip to the town library. There he found a colorful picture book about the planets and stars. Thumbing through it, he came to an article about Mars, with a photo of the "red planet" taken by one of the larger telescopes of the day. The article explained that in the 1870s an Italian astronomer had claimed to have seen "canals" on Mars. In the 1890s American astronomer Percival Lowell had decided to devote his career to studying the planet. Lowell became convinced that the canals seen earlier had been built by intelligent beings.

This was all new information to young Bob Williams. Put simply, he later recalled, "I was gaga!

A young Bob Williams (center), his brother Ken (right), and friend Ken Kuskey built a small planetarium for a California Boy Scout Scoutorama in 1957.

Rushing home, I found a magnifying glass and tried to see further details in the article's photos of Mars. Of course, all I could make out were masses of tiny colored pixels!"

But his momentary disappointment didn't matter, because by then Williams was hooked. He later described having a personal transformation: "I found myself freaking out over astronomy. In that one day at age 12, I made the life decision to become an astronomer, and thereafter I never deviated from that path for a single moment."

During high school Williams read every book about astronomy he could find, obtained a small telescope, and spent many nights outside gazing at the night sky. After he graduated, his astronomical journey continued at the University of California in Berkeley, where he earned a bachelor's degree. Then he got a PhD in astronomy at the University of Wisconsin in Madison. For 18 years, Williams taught astronomy at the University of Arizona in Tucson. In 1985 he became director of the Cerro Tololo Inter-American Observatory in Chile, the chief U.S. observatory in the southern hemisphere. Williams returned to the United States in 1993 to take the job of director of the Space Telescope Science Institute.

During these many years of distinguished work as an astronomer, Williams particularly studied how galaxies are formed and how they change. His interests and expertise paralleled those of one of his idols—Edwin Hubble. It seemed only natural, therefore, that after becoming head of the STScI he would think about using the new space telescope to take pictures of distant galaxies. He was not totally certain that photographing a seemingly blank patch of sky in Ursa Major would reveal images of galaxies whose light had set out for Earth many billions of years before. But he knew he had to take the chance.

A member of Williams' team, Harry Ferguson, agreed that they must take the chance. Nevertheless,

Astronomers Harry Ferguson (from left), Mark Dickinson, and Bob Williams met often in the Space Telescope Science Institute library to plan the Hubble Deep Field project.

like Williams, he realized that it was a big risk. Much more certain, Ferguson felt, was the fact that if they were successful, the ground-breaking photo and the instrument that had taken it would historically be forever linked. "One of the great legacies of the Hubble Telescope," he said with a hint of hope, "will be these deep images of the sky showing galaxies to the faintest possible limits with the greatest possible clarity from here out to the very horizon of the universe."

ChapterThree
WHAT HUBBLE DEEP FIELD SHOWS

The 10 days from December 18 to 28, 1995, were highly eventful for Bob Williams and the members of his team. They relentlessly and carefully guided and monitored the orbiting Hubble Space Telescope as it sped around Earth many times each day. All the while, its wide-field camera took one photo after another of the tiny target area in the Big Bear constellation.

The more than 300 images they took, which later would be combined into a single one, had various exposure times. Sometimes the camera focused on the target for as few as 15 minutes; at other times it lingered for as many as 40 minutes. Another way the images varied was in their colors. The scientists directed the camera to use an array of colored filters, including those for red, blue, and infrared light. Williams later recalled, "These were later digitally combined to produce a single image having hues the human eye sees as faithful colors."

When those 10 historic days ended and the team combined the preliminary images into the final photo, everyone agreed that the results were astonishing. As a science journalist later remarked, "To say it was a triumph would be an understatement." Even Williams, who had been more optimistic than most

The stunning deep field photo was assembled from separate images taken in infrared, blue, and red light.

experts about what to expect, could barely contain his enthusiasm.

The team released the photo two weeks later, on January 15, 1996. The waiting press and public finally learned what had so excited the picture's creators. They had launched the experiment hoping to capture at least a few images of very distant galaxies, but they had succeeded far beyond that modest expectation. Astronomer Robert Kirshner, who had firmly opposed the project, fittingly summed up what the image showed. "Almost everything in the Hubble Deep Field image is a galaxy!" he said with a touch of awe. "Galaxies in the foreground overlap with galaxies in the background until the Hubble Deep Field begins to show wall-to-wall galaxies!"

The first estimates at this early stage of studying the Hubble Deep Field suggested that it showed at least 1,500 galaxies and possibly as many as 3,000. The faintest objects visible to the unaided human eye are still 4 billion times as bright as the galaxies observed by Hubble. The fact that so many galaxies existed in that single small corner of the night sky spoke volumes about galactic numbers in general. "One thing was stunningly clear: with this achievement, the estimated number of galaxies in the universe had multiplied enormously—to 50 billion, five times as many as previously estimated," reported science journalist John Noble Wilford in *The New York Times*.

Another unexpected and fascinating finding of the project was the great number of galactic shapes. "The variety of galaxies we see is amazing," Williams said. There were several of the familiar spiral galaxies that looked like the Andromeda galaxy, the Milky Way's nearby neighbor. Andromeda's image

"Galaxies in the foreground overlap with galaxies in the background until the Hubble Deep Field begins to show wall-to-wall galaxies!"

The Andromeda galaxy is the most far away thing people can see with the unaided eye. It appears as a smudge of light in the night sky.

is familiar to many through articles and books. The Hubble Deep Field also contained round-shaped galaxies and many irregularly shaped ones.

Williams and other astronomers suspected that some galaxies were in the early stages of their formation. That's because the Hubble Deep Field photo acts in part like a cosmic time machine. As explained by science writer Mark Sullivan, "The further away a galaxy is, the longer it has taken light to reach us—and the earlier in the universe we are looking. Since that light was emitted the universe has continued to expand. Some galaxies in the picture lie close to the edge of the observable universe. This is the furthest point in space to which we could, in principle, see." That point, astronomers say, is about 13.8 billion light-years from Earth—light from objects more distant than that has not yet had enough time to reach our planet.

So people who look at the Hubble Deep Field are seeing galaxies several billion years after they formed in the period following the Big Bang. As Williams put it, "We are clearly seeing some of the galaxies as they were more than 10 billion years ago, in the process of formation." Kirshner agreed. He said that the Hubble Deep Field showed clearly that "when the galaxies were young, they were very irregular. They were having collisions, they were erupting, they were having adolescent outbursts."

Kirshner also had the grace to admit he had been mistaken in urging Williams not to pursue the project. "Bob was right, I was wrong," he said. Williams' decision to use his discretionary time on the Hubble telescope, Kirshner said, "was a courageous thing."

Williams, Kirshner, and other astronomers recognized that the Hubble Deep Field image contained within it important clues about galaxy formation in the early universe. It was not merely a question of seeing back in time and seeing what

ACCELERATING UNIVERSE

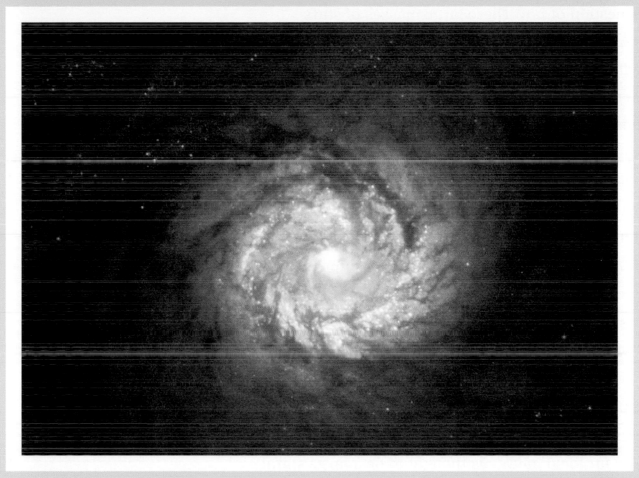

Hubble took a sharp image of Messier 61, a starburst galaxy known for its very high rate of star formation.

In addition to their other scientific benefits, Hubble's images of distant galaxies have helped to elaborate on the answer to an old question posed by astronomers. Namely, would the universe's galaxies and other matter keep expanding forever? Or would they slow down and collapse back into a very dense object like the one that exploded in the Big Bang? Astronomers called the theoretical end point the Big Crunch. By the close of the 20th century, scientists generally agreed that the expansion of the universe would never end.

In 2011, however, three astrophysicists—Saul Perlmutter, Brian Schmidt, and Adam Riess—won the Nobel Prize for showing there was more to it than that.

By studying the light from several very distant galaxies, they determined something astonishing. The universe is not only expanding, but that expansion is increasing at a faster and faster rate. Scientists wonder what is causing the acceleration and call the force "dark energy."

"All we can say is that there's an entity that is forcing the universe to accelerate outside of the wishes of gravity," said astrophysicist Neil deGrasse Tyson, director of the Hayden Planetarium at the American Museum of Natural History. "The term 'dark energy' seems apt, but we don't know what it is—that remains a mystery. The Nobel is for the discovery of this mystery."

very early galaxies looked like. There was also the question of how these large masses of stars assembled in the first place. The simplest idea is that gravity caused one huge cloud of gas to collapse and form the stars within a galaxy. Or many smaller clouds could have collapsed and formed stars first—called protogalaxies—and then have been pulled together to build up a typically sized galaxy.

Also, once they have formed, how do galaxies maintain their populations of stars? Do they mostly pull in existing stars from outside their limits, or do they create new stars from gases floating within?

Before Williams and his associates created the Hubble Deep Field, most of what astronomers thought they knew about galaxy formation consisted of educated guesses. These were based on observing existing, older galaxies, including the Milky Way itself. Our local galaxy is thought to be a large spiral very similar in shape and size to the Andromeda galaxy. The two are sometimes referred to as sister galaxies. As part of the initial 1996 news release about the Hubble Deep Field, a NASA spokesperson summed up the then prevailing assumptions for how the Milky Way formed. "Detailed studies of the ages and chemical compositions of stars in our own galaxy," said Ray Villard, "suggest that it has led a relatively quiet existence, forming stars at a rate of a few suns a year for the last 10 billion years.

Present Milky Way

Early Milky Way

An artist's illustration (bottom) of the early Milky Way is based on Hubble studies.

Other spiral galaxies seem to have similar histories. If this is typical evolution for spiral galaxies, then predictions can be made for what they should have

looked like at half their present age—including their size, color and abundance."

In other words, theories for how spiral galaxies formed might be tested at least partly by studying some galactic images in the Hubble Deep Field. The fact that it looks back in time is crucially important. Some of the oddly shaped galaxies in the photo, which were quite young when their light began

Hubble photographed NGC 3344, a spiral galaxy about half the size of the Milky Way. It is about 25 million light-years away.

The operations team at NASA's Goddard Space Flight Center monitors the Hubble Space Telescope.

moving toward Earth, could conceivably be early groups of stars that would eventually become spiral galaxies. Maybe, some scientists suggested, the Milky Way looked like one of these oddly shaped blobs of stars 10 billion or 12 billion years ago, before developing into its current spiral shape.

As John Wilford pointed out, astronomers expected "that more detailed analysis of these pictures and further Hubble photography of the same region, combined with observations by some of the world's most powerful ground-based telescopes, should lead to a better understanding of how galaxies form and evolve and when these processes began in the young universe." That is, when people look at the photo Williams and his colleagues took, how far back

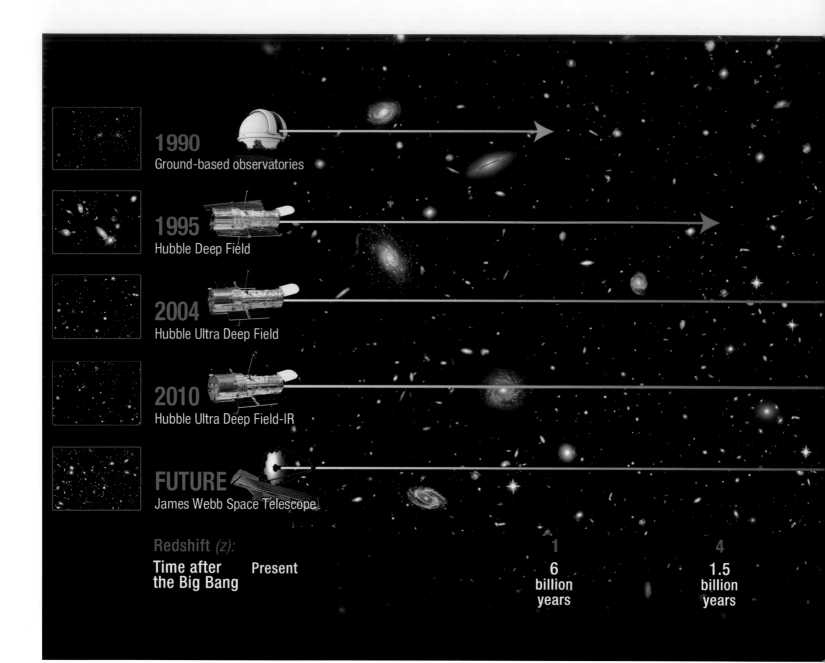

1990
Ground-based observatories

1995
Hubble Deep Field

2004
Hubble Ultra Deep Field

2010
Hubble Ultra Deep Field-IR

FUTURE
James Webb Space Telescope

Redshift (z):   1   4
Time after   Present   6   1.5
the Big Bang   billion   billion
                                                 years   years

in time are they seeing? "The researchers likened their achievement to an archeological dig," Wilford wrote. "In particular, they compared it to archeologists' finding ruins of a royal city, sensing they have something big but not knowing its age."

6 7 8 10 >20

800 million years

480 million years

200 million years

Hubble revolutionized the study of the early universe. Before it was launched, ground-based telescopes were able to observe about halfway back through cosmic history. Hubble's latest instrument can see about 96 percent of the way back to the Big Bang.

The primary question about age, Williams himself realized, was this: How long after the Big Bang did the scene in the Hubble Deep Field snapshot exist? Clearly, he realized, enough time had gone by for thousands of galaxies to form or begin forming. How long had that process taken? Exact figures for the universe's age remain elusive. But astronomers using the Hubble Space Telescope continue to search for answers.

ChapterFour
NEW LEVEL OF COSMIC IMMENSITY

When Bob Williams and his team released the Hubble Deep Field photo in January 1996, its impact was immediate. Tony Darnell, who runs an astronomy website, summed up the sheer brilliance of the photo as a technical accomplishment. "The Hubble Space Telescope stared for 10 days at a rather unremarkable patch of sky. The results were nothing less than humbling on a universal scale," he said. "Thousands of galaxies filled the image. Roughly 3,000 galaxies were detected in a patch of sky that looks completely and utterly empty."

Astronomer Patrick McCarthy echoed the same sentiment, adding some crucial details. The Hubble Deep Field "changed scientists' view of the universe by revealing a rich tapestry of galaxies with shapes and structures foreign to the galaxy shapes that are seen in the universe today," he said. "Many are in the throes of violent collisions and mergers that may transform them from one type of galaxy—such as spirals like the Milky Way—into other types."

On a more personal level, Darnell noted, the image could capture the imaginations of scientists and non-scientists alike. Putting aside his own interests in astronomy, he said, the photo had touched him on what he could only describe as the gut level.

The sharpest image of the Orion nebula—the closest star-forming region to Earth—was made with data from Hubble's camera.

When the average person learns how far away even the nearest stars are to the sun and Earth, the tremendous size of the local galaxy—the Milky Way—becomes apparent and impressive. Yet the

Hubble Deep Field, Darnell said, with its array of extremely distant galaxies, carries the viewer to a new and shattering level of cosmic immensity. "For the first time," he said, "I got a real feeling for just how immense the universe actually is. It's absolutely mind-blowing if you stop to think about it, that by looking at a patch of sky that appears to have nothing in it, and you stare at it long enough, you see an image full of galaxies."

While praising the Hubble Deep Field, scientists have emphasized that it was far from the last word. Although stunning and informative, it did not answer all the questions astronomers had long been asking about distant galaxies and the structure of the universe. Rather, it acted as a starting point in scientific discussions about galaxy formation in the early cosmos.

The image prompted a huge number of discussions. Astronomers and other scientists speculated about the universe's size, shape, and age based on the results of the Hubble Deep Field project. A recent count found that nearly 1,000 scientific papers and articles had mentioned the 1996 *Astronomical Journal* article in which Bob Williams and his assistants had presented the Hubble Deep Field's first findings.

The discussions triggered by the image covered a wide range of concepts, all either directly or

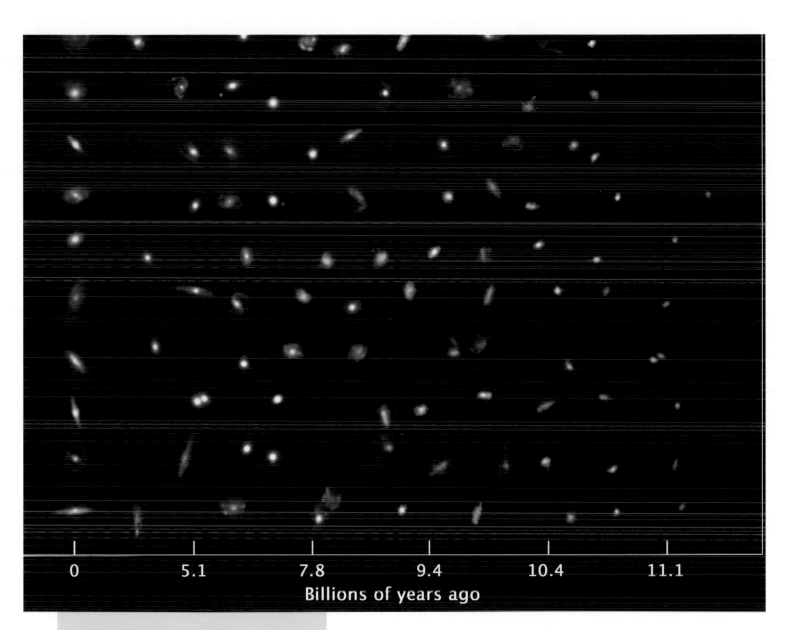

0   5.1   7.8   9.4   10.4   11.1

Billions of years ago

Hubble images helped scientists plot the age of galaxies similar to the Milky Way. This composite image features galaxies at various stages of construction. The galaxies on the far right existed when the universe was about 2 billion years old.

indirectly connected to galaxies. Their formation when the universe was still young was a major topic of debate, as was the galaxies' evolution and their relationship to the structure of the cosmos.

The Space Telescope Science Institute explained how the 1995 Hubble Deep Field and more recent photography projects made serious discussions of such topics possible. "Before Hubble was launched in 1990, astronomers could barely see normal galaxies to 7 billion years ago," said an institute article in an astronomy magazine. "Observations with telescopes on the ground were not able to establish how galaxies formed and evolved in the early universe. Hubble gave astronomers their first view of the actual forms and shapes of galaxies when they were young. This provided compelling, direct visual evidence that the universe is truly changing as it ages. Like watching individual frames of a motion picture, the Hubble deep surveys reveal the emergence of structure in the infant universe and the subsequent dynamic stages of galaxy evolution."

The 1995 Hubble Deep Field laid the groundwork for similar projects. The later versions took full advantage of the latest improvements in telescope and camera technology.

The first of the Deep Field follow-up photo projects, which also were supervised by Bob Williams, was done in October 1998. "I had wanted to undertake a second Deep Field shortly after the first," Williams later explained. "When it became evident within a few months that researchers were drawing important conclusions from the data about the history of galaxy formation, I knew then that we had to conduct another Deep Field in a different area of the sky."

"Hubble gave astronomers their first view of the actual forms and shapes of galaxies when they were young."

13 MILLION PATCHES OF SKY

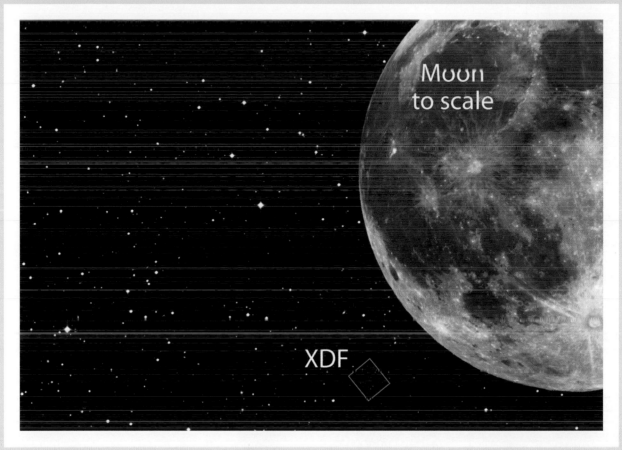

A NASA illustration compares the size of Hubble's eXtreme Deep Field to the size of the full moon.

The Hubble Deep Field, Hubble Ultra Deep Field, and other striking images of groups of distant galaxies taken by the Hubble Space Telescope each covered a tiny patch of the night sky. In each case the width of the image was equal to a small fraction of the diameter of the full moon.

Astronomers measure these and other parts of the night sky in units that correspond to degrees and fractions of degrees. The entire sky is 360 degrees in circumference. Smaller units include arc minutes, each measuring one-60th of a degree, and arc seconds, each measuring one-60th of an arc minute. The Space Telescope Science Institute reported that the Hubble Ultra Deep Field covered about 11.5 square arc minutes of sky. Complex math calculations show that the entire night sky contains close to 13 million patches of sky that size. To be exact, it would take 12,913,983 images the size of the Hubble Ultra Deep Field to cover the whole night sky.

"It is easy to get lost" in such big numbers, says Ryan Anderson of the U.S. Geological Survey. "They are so overwhelmingly huge that the human mind cannot rationalize them. But at the very least, we can get a sense of things. The Ultra Deep Field shows us just how big the universe is and how small and fragile we all are."

This time Williams and his team targeted an area of the southern sky. They chose a tiny patch of sky in the constellation Tucana, near the southern celestial pole—the imaginary point above Earth's south pole. Taking the separate exposures that were needed to assemble the final picture—officially known as the Hubble Deep Field South—required using the Hubble

Against a background of thousands of galaxies, a galaxy with a long streamer of stars appears to race through space in a 2002 image taken by Hubble.

Space Telescope for 177 of its orbits over a 10-day period. The stunning result captured the images of an estimated 2,500 distant galaxies.

Next came the Hubble Ultra Deep Field, in 2004. By this time the Hubble Space Telescope had been equipped with new and more sensitive cameras. Focusing on a target region in Fornax (the Furnace), a constellation below the larger and more famous Orion (the Hunter), the Hubble Ultra Deep Field required a record-setting 400 orbits of the Hubble

The Hubble Ultra Deep Field image was further refined in 2014 with the addition of ultraviolet light data to study distant galaxies.

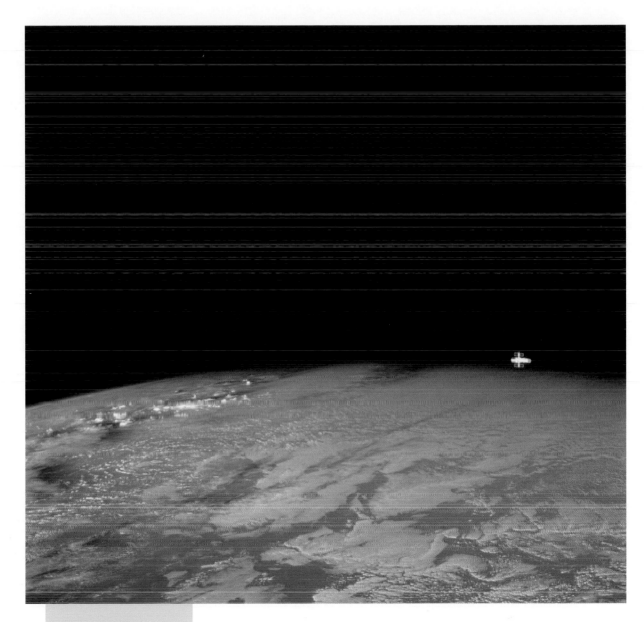

The Hubble Space Telescope appears to hover over the edge of Earth in a 2002 photo taken from the space shuttle *Columbia*.

Space Telescope. The new image, a combination of 800 separate exposures, revealed about 10,000 separate galaxies. The project's greatest achievement was to show astronomers what the galaxies looked like a mere 400 million to 800 million years after the Big Bang. At that point, it appears, galaxies were a fairly new phenomenon, and they were still undergoing the violent changes of initial formation. The Hubble Ultra Deep Field, according to NASA, "is studded with a wide range of galaxies of various sizes, shapes, and colors. In vibrant contrast to the image's rich harvest of classic spiral and elliptical galaxies, there is a zoo of oddball galaxies littering the field. Some look like toothpicks; others like links on a bracelet. A few appear to be interacting. Their strange shapes are a far cry from the majestic spiral and elliptical galaxies we see today. These oddball galaxies chronicle a period when the universe was more chaotic. Order and structure were just beginning to emerge."

Still another Deep Field Project came in 2009. Its team focused on the same area in Fornax that had been the target of the 2004 Ultra Deep Field. This time, however, astronomers had the advantage of a new camera mounted on the Hubble Space Telescope. It takes pictures in the infrared section of the spectrum, which lets scientists see much fainter galaxies than ever before.

Several years later, in 2012, NASA released yet another image. This one, called Hubble eXtreme Deep Field, added more data to the earlier images. "Magnificent spiral galaxies similar in shape to our Milky Way and the neighboring Andromeda galaxy appear in this image, as do the large, fuzzy red galaxies where the formation of new stars has

"These oddball galaxies chronicle a period when the universe was more chaotic. Order and structure were just beginning to emerge."

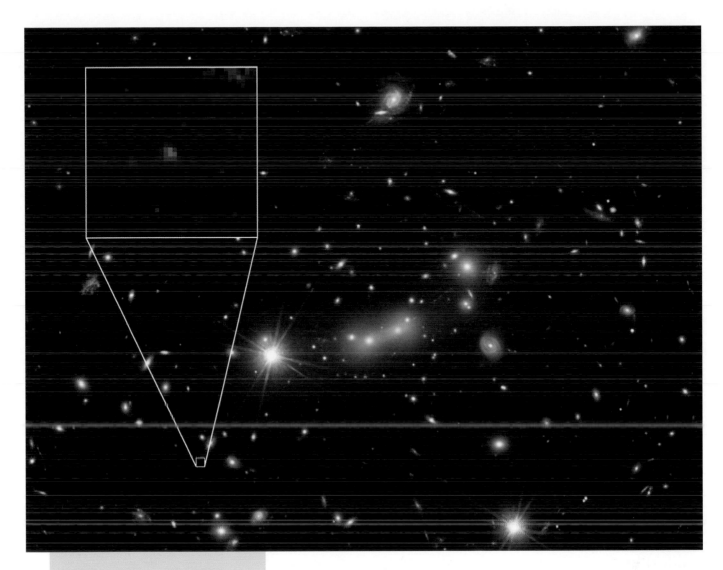

Astronomers in 2011 used the Hubble Space Telescope to uncover the farthest known galaxy in the universe. The inset contains a close-up of the young dwarf galaxy. It is seen 420 million years after the Big Bang when the universe was 3 percent of its present age of 13.8 billion years old.

ceased," said a NASA press release. "These red galaxies are the remnants of dramatic collisions between galaxies and are in their declining years. Peppered across the field are tiny, faint, more distant galaxies that were like the seedlings from which today's striking galaxies grew. The history of galaxies — from soon after the first galaxies were born to the great galaxies of today, like our Milky Way—is laid out in this one remarkable image."

The Hubble Deep Field South and Hubble Ultra Deep Field are among more than half a dozen Deep Field projects undertaken by NASA since the original project in 1995. That pioneering image opened up a vast array of distant galaxies for astronomers to study in relation to the universe's earliest years. Each new Deep Field project has further advanced what is known about galaxies.

The next advancement will come in October 2018 when the James Webb Space Telescope—sponsored and built through a collaboration of NASA, the Canadian Space Agency, and the European Space Agency—is expected to launch. The new space telescope, named after former NASA Administrator James E. Webb, is much larger and more powerful than the Hubble telescope, which remains in operation. Hubble has a mirror almost 8 feet (2.4 m) across. The new space telescope's mirror, which will collect infrared light, is a whopping 21 feet (6.5 m) in diameter.

The James Webb Space Telescope "represents just as big a step up from Hubble as Hubble was from ground-based telescopes," said astrophysicist Ethan Siegel. "Hubble taught us what our universe looks like; James Webb will teach us how our universe came to be this way."

A Hubble image of a galaxy 4 billion light-years away gives a sneak peek of the early universe and a taste of what the new James Webb Space Telescope will reveal in even more detail.

Timeline

1889

Edwin Hubble, who will become one of the 20th century's greatest astronomers, is born

1922–1923

Edwin Hubble detects individual stars within several nebulae, leading him to conclude that nebulae are separate galaxies

1923

German scientist Hermann Oberth describes the possible benefits of an orbiting space telescope

1949

Astronomer Fred Hoyle coins the term "Big Bang" to describe the giant explosion that most astronomers think created the universe

1953

Edwin Hubble dies

1940

Robert Williams, who will become an astronomer and lead the team that creates the Hubble Deep Field, is born

1948

The 200-inch (5-m) Hale Telescope, on California's Mount Palomar, then the world's most powerful telescope, begins operation

1972

Orbiting U.S. astronauts snap the photo of Earth that will become widely famous as the Blue Marble

1977

Congress approves spending money to build the Hubble Space Telescope

1979

The multiple-mirror telescope at Whipple Observatory in Arizona begins operation

Timeline

1985

Williams becomes director of the Cerro Tololo Inter-American Observatory in Chile

1990

The Hubble Space Telescope is launched into orbit

1995

A team of scientists led by astronomer Williams creates the Hubble Deep Field image

2004

A team of scientists produces the Hubble Ultra Deep Field

2009

The Hubble Ultra Deep Field 09 uses a new camera to make observations much deeper into longer wavelength infrared light

1996

The W.M. Keck twin telescopes begin operation in Hawaii

1998

Williams and his team create the Hubble Deep Field South

2012

NASA announces the creation of the Hubble eXtreme Deep Field

2016

The Hubble Frontier Fields project captures six new deep fields to expand the area covered by distant galaxy observations

Glossary

Big Bang—theory that the universe began about 14 billion years ago in an explosion; space, matter, energy, and even time itself were created together; it started an expansion of the universe that continues today

celestial—of or relating to the sky

continuous viewing zone—place in the sky where an orbiting telescope takes photos without Earth's getting in the way

cosmic—having to do with the universe

cosmos—universe

elliptical galaxy—galaxy having a somewhat roundish shape and little or no visible structure

exposure time—the length of time a camera shutter is open to expose light to the camera's sensor

galactic—having to do with galaxies

galaxy—cluster of millions or billions of stars, together with gas and dust, bound together by gravity

infrared—invisible light waves a little longer than the red light waves on the visible light spectrum

nebulae—huge clouds of gas and dust in space; from a Latin word meaning "mist" or "cloud"

spiral galaxy—galaxy with spiral arms and a well-defined internal structure

universe—all matter and energy, including Earth, galaxies, and contents of space

Additional Resources

Further Reading

Bortz, Fred. *The Big Bang Theory: Edwin Hubble and the Origins of the Universe.*
New York: Rosen Publishing, 2014.

Cole, Michael D. *Eye on the Universe: The Incredible Hubble Space Telescope.*
Berkeley Heights, N.J.: Enslow Publishers, 2013.

Dickinson, Terence. *Hubble's Universe: Greatest Discoveries and Latest Images.*
Buffalo, N.Y.: Firefly Books Ltd., 2014.

Peterson, Carolyn Collins. *Astronomy 101: From the Sun and Moon to Wormholes and Warp Drive, Key Theories, Discoveries, and Facts About the Universe.*
Avon, Mass.: Adams Media, 2013.

Internet Sites

Use FactHound to find Internet sites related to this book.
Visit *www.facthound.com*
Just type in 9780756556433 and go.

Critical Thinking Questions

As he prepared to take the Hubble Deep Field image, several of astronomer Bob Williams' colleagues urged him not to go forward with the project. What led them to have this negative attitude? Detail the reasons some of them later changed their minds.

Before Edwin Hubble began working with the Hooker Telescope atop Mount Wilson, how did he and other astronomers interpret the nebulae they saw in the sky? How did his work redefine the nebulae and show that the universe is far larger than previously thought?

Explain why the Hubble Deep Field is a kind of time machine that allows humans to gaze far into the past.

Source Notes

Page 10, col. 2, line 15: NASA. "About the Hubble Space Telescope." *Hubble 2010: Science Year in Review*, pp. 22-23. 30 Nov. 2016. http://hubblesite.org/hubble_discoveries/science_year_in_review/pdf/2010/about_the_hubble_space_telescope.pdf

Page 11, line 1: Bob Williams. Phone interview. 9 Sept. 2016.

Page 11, line 11: Ibid.

Page 12, line 9: Drake, Nadia. "When Hubble Stared at Nothing for 100 Hours." *National Geographic.* 24 April 2015. 30 Nov. 2016. http://phenomena.nationalgeographic.com/2015/04/24/when-hubble-stared-at-nothing-for-100-hours/

Page 13, line 5: Tony Darnell. "The Hubble Deep Field: The Most Important Image Ever Taken." *Deep Astronomy.* 6 Sept. 2006. 30 Nov. 2016. http://deepastronomy.com/article/15/hubble-deep-field

Page 20, line 11: Christen Browniee. "Hubble's Guide to the Expanding Universe." Classics of the Scientific Literature." Proceedings of the National Academy of Sciences in the United States of America. 30 Nov. 2016. http://www.pnas.org/site/classics/classics2.xhtml

Page 20, line 25: William Sheehan and Christopher J. Conselice. *Galactic Encounters: Our Majestic and Evolving Star-System, from the Big Bang to Time's End.* New York: Springer, 2014, p. 346.

Page 26, line 29: Bob Williams. Phone interview.

Page 27, line 7: Ibid.

Page 29, line 5: NASA Newscenter. "Hubble's Deepest View of the Universe Unveils Bewildering Galaxies Across Billions of Years." Hubblesite. 15 Jan. 1996. 30 Nov. 2016. http://hubblesite.org/newscenter/archive/releases/1996/01/text/

Page 30, line 17: Bob Williams. Phone interview.

Page 30, line 23: "When Hubble Stared at Nothing for 100 Hours."

Page 32, line 4: Robert P. Kirshner. *The Extravagant Universe: Exploding Stars, Dark Energy, and the Accelerating Cosmos.* Princeton, N.J.: Princeton University Press, 2002, p. 12.

Page 32, line 17: John Noble Wilford. "Space Telescope Reveals 40 Billion More Galaxies." *The New York Times*, p. 1. 1 Jan. 1996.

Page 32, line 25: "Hubble's Deepest View of the Universe Unveils Bewildering Galaxies Across Billions of Years."

Page 33, line 8: Mark Sullivan. "Hubble's deep field images of the early universe are postcards from billions of years ago." *The Conversation.* 24 April 2015. 30 Nov. 2016. http://phys.org/news/2015-04-hubble-deep-field-images-early.html

Page 34, line 11: "Hubble's Deepest View of the Universe Unveils Bewildering Galaxies across Billions of Years."

Page 34, line 14: "When Hubble Stared at Nothing for 100 Hours."

Page 34, line 20: Ibid.

Page 35, col. 2, line 6: Clara Moskowitz. "Nobel Prize 'Inevitable' for Accelerating Universe Discovery, Physicists Say." Space.com. 4 Oct. 2011. 19 April 2017. http://www.space.com/13177-nobel-prize-accelerating-universe-dark-energy-reaction.html

Page 36, line 24: "Hubble's Deepest View of the Universe Unveils Bewildering Galaxies across Billions of Years."

Page 39, line 8: "Space Telescope Reveals 40 Billion More Galaxies."

Page 40, line 1: Ibid.

Page 42, line 5: "The Hubble Deep Field: The Most Important Image Ever Taken."

Page 42, line 14: Patrick McCarthy. "Nearly a Century Later, Edwin Hubble's Legacy Lives On." Space.com. 17 June 2014. 30 Nov. 2016. http://www.space.com/26269-giant-telescopes-revealing-13-billion-year-history.html

Page 44, line 3: "The Hubble Deep Field: The Most Important Image Ever Taken."

Page 46, line 1: "Hubble Goes to the eXtreme to Assemble Farthest Ever View of the Universe." Hubblesite. 25 Sept. 2012. 30 Nov. 2016. http://hubblesite.org/newscenter/archive/releases/2012/37/image/a/

Page 46, line 21: NASA Newscenter. "The Universe 'Down Under' is the Latest Target for Hubble's Latest Deep-View." Hubblesite. 23 Nov. 1998. 30 Nov. 2016. http://hubblesite.org/newscenter/archive/releases/1998/41/background/

Page 47, col. 2, line 7: Ryan Anderson. "How big is the Hubble Ultra Deep Field image?" Ask an Astronomer. Astronomy Department. Cornell University. 30 Nov. 2016. http://curious.astro.cornell.edu/about-us/98-the-universe/galaxies/observing-galaxies/535-how-big-is-the-hubble-ultra-deep-field-image-intermediate

Page 52, line 3: NASA Newscenter. "Hubble's Deepest View Ever of the Universe Unveils Earliest Galaxies." Hubblesite. 9 March 2004. 30 Nov. 2016. http://hubblesite.org/newscenter/archive/releases/2004/07/text/

Page 52, line 25: NASA Newscenter. "Hubble Goes to the eXtreme to Assemble Farthest Ever View of the Universe." Hubblesite. 25 Sept. 2012. 30 Nov. 2016. http://hubblesite.org/newscenter/archive/releases/2012/37/image/a/

Page 54, line 21: Ethan Siegel. "How NASA's James Webb Space Telescope Will Answer Astronomy's Biggest Questions." *Forbes.* 1 March 2017. 2 March 2017. https://www.forbes.com/sites/startswithabang/2017/01/18/a-behind-the-scenes-look-at-building-the-greatest-space-telescope-of-all/

Select Bibliography

"The 200-inch (5.1 meter) Hale Telescope." Palomar Observatory. 12 Aug. 2016. 30 Nov. 2016. http://www.astro.caltech.edu/palomar/about/telescopes/hale.html

Bolden, Charles F., Jr., Owen Edwards, John Mace Grunsfeld, and Zoltan Levay. *Expanding Universe: Photographs from the Hubble Space Telescope*. Koln, Germany: Taschen, 2015.

Darnell, Tony. "The Hubble Deep Field: The Most Important Image Ever Taken." *Deep Astronomy*. 6 Sept. 2006. 30 Nov. 2016. http://deepastronomy.com/article/15/hubble-deep-field

Drake, Nadia. "When Hubble Stared at Nothing for 100 Hours." *National Geographic*. 24 April 2015. 30 Nov. 2016. http://phenomena.nationalgeographic.com/2015/04/24/when-hubble-stared-at-nothing-for-100-hours/

"Edwin Hubble and the Expanding Universe." Australia Telescope National Facility. 30 Nov. 2016. http://www.atnf.csiro.au/outreach/education/senior/cosmicengine/hubble.html

"Galaxies, Clusters, and Superclusters." *Runaway Universe*. NOVA Online. PBS. November 2000. 30 Nov. 2016. http://www.pbs.org/wgbh/nova/universe/tour_ggs.html#n05

Geach, James. *Galaxy: Mapping the Cosmos*. London: Reaktion Books, 2015.

Goldsmith, Donald. *The Runaway Universe: The Race to Find the Future of the Cosmos*. Cambridge, Mass.: Perseus Books, 2000.

Hawking, Stephen, and Leonard Mlodinow. *The Grand Design*. New York: Bantam Books, 2010.

Hawking, Stephen. *The Universe in a Nutshell*. New York: Bantam Books, 2001.

"History of the Telescope." The MMT Observatory. 30 Nov. 2016. https://www.mmto.org/node/6

Hubble, Edwin. "The Problem of the Ever Expanding Universe." *American Scientist*, Vol. 30, No. 2, April 1942. 30 Nov. 2016. http://nimble.nimblebrain.net/hubblepaper.html

Hubble, Edwin. *The Realm of the Nebulae*. New Haven: Yale University Press, 1936.

"The Hubble Story." Hubble Space Telescope. 30 Nov. 2016. http://www.nasa.gov/mission_pages/hubble/story/the_story.html

"Hubble Ultra Deep Field 2009 Detects Earliest Galaxies." *Astronomy*. 6 Jan. 2010. 30 Nov. 2016. http://www.astronomy.com/news/2010/01/hubble-ultra-deep-field-2009-detects-earliest-galaxies

"Hubble unveils a deep sea of small and faint early galaxies." *Astronomy*. 7 Jan. 2014. 30 Nov. 2016. http://www.astronomy.com/news/2014/01/hubble-unveils-a-deep-sea-of-small-and-faint-early-galaxies

Jones, Mark H., Robert J. A. Lambourne, and Stephen Sarjeant, eds. *An Introduction to Galaxies and Cosmology*. Cambridge: Cambridge University Press, 2015.

King, Gilbert. "How Edwin Hubble Became the 20th Century's Greatest Astronomer." *Smithsonian*. 20 May 2013. 30 Nov. 2016. http://www.smithsonianmag.com/history/how-edwin-hubble-became-the-20th-centurys-greatest-astronomer-66148381/?no-ist

Kirshner, Robert P. *The Extravagant Universe: Exploding Stars, Dark Energy, and the Accelerating Cosmos*. Princeton, N.J.: Princeton University Press, 2002.

NASA. "About the Hubble Space Telescope." *Hubble 2010: Science Year in Review*. 30 Nov. 2016. http://hubblesite.org/hubble_discoveries/science_year_in_review/pdf/2010/about_the_hubble_space_telescope.pdf

NASA Headquarters. "Hubble provides first census of galaxies near cosmic dawn." *Astronomy*. 12 Dec. 2012. 30 Nov. 2016. http://www.astronomy.com/news/2012/12/hubble-provides-first-census-of-galaxies-near-cosmic-dawn

NASA Newscenter. "Hubble's Deepest View of the Universe Unveils Bewildering Galaxies Across Billions of Years." Hubblesite. 15 Jan. 1996. 30 Nov. 2016. http://hubblesite.org/newscenter/archive/releases/1996/01/text/

NASA Newscenter. "Hubble Goes to the eXtreme to Assemble Farthest Ever View of the Universe." Hubblesite. 25 Sept. 2012. 30 Nov. 2016. http://hubblesite.org/newscenter/archive/releases/2012/37/image/a/

Sheehan, William, and Christopher J. Conselice. *Galactic Encounters: Our Majestic and Evolving Star-System, from the Big Bang to Time's End*. New York: Springer, 2014.

Tyson, Neil deGrasse, and Donald Goldsmith. *Fourteen Billion Years of Cosmic Evolution*. New York: W.W. Norton & Co., 2014.

"Universe Timeline." *Runaway Universe*. NOVA Online. PBS. November 2000. 30 Nov. 2016. http://www.pbs.org/wgbh/nova/universe/historysans.html

Weiler, Edward. *Hubble: A Journey Through Space and Time*. New York: Abrams, 2010.

Wilford, John Noble. "Space Telescope Reveals 40 Billion More Galaxies." *The New York Times*. 1 Jan. 1996. 30 Nov. 2016. http://www.nytimes.com/1996/01/16/science/space-telescope-reveals-40-billion-more-galaxies.html?_r=1

Index

About the Author

Historian and award-winning author Don Nardo has written many books for young people. He lives with his wife, Christine, in Massachusetts.